Published in Great Britain in MMXIII by
Book House, an imprint of
The Salariya Book Company Ltd
25 Marlborough Place, Brighton BN1 1UB
www.salariya.com
www.book-house.co.uk

PB ISBN-13: 978-1-908759-92-4

1 3 5 7 9 8 6 4 2

A CIP catalogue record for this book is available
from the British Library.
Printed and bound in China.
Printed on paper from sustainable sources.

Visit our website at **www.book-house.co.uk**
or go to **www.salariya.com**
for **free** electronic versions of:
You Wouldn't Want to be an Egyptian Mummy!
You Wouldn't Want to be a Roman Gladiator!
You Wouldn't Want to be a Polar Explorer!
You Wouldn't Want to Sail on a 19th-Century Whaling Ship!

Visit our **new** online shop at
shop.salariya.com
for great offers, gift ideas, all our new releases
and free postage and packaging.

CHRISTMAS

A VERY PECULIAR HISTORY

QUIZ BOOK

With lashings of
second helpings

CONTENTS

CHRISTMAS AROUND THE WORLD

Q1

THE ISLANDERS OF ORKNEY CELEBRATED 'SOW NIGHT' ON 17 DECEMBER UNTIL THE 20TH CENTURY, BUT WHAT WAS IT?

a) They took to the fields to sow seeds of their crops.
b) They killed a pig and feasted on it.
c) All the pigs of the islands were allowed to run free.
d) There was a pedigree sow competition.

Q2

IN SOUTHERN FRANCE, HOW MANY TIMES DOES THE YULE LOG HAVE TO BE CARRIED AROUND A HOUSE BEFORE IT CAN BE BURNT?

a) Once
b) Three times
c) Five times
d) Twelve times

TV TRADITION

STRANGE BUT TRUE. ONE OF THE MOST POPULAR US CHRISTMAS TV BROADCASTS IS A THREE-HOUR FILM — OF A FIREPLACE! THIS IS NOT, HOWEVER, AN ORDINARY, EVERYDAY CHIMNEY. IT STANDS IN THE HOME OF NEW YORK'S LORD MAYOR, IS HUNG WITH CHRISTMAS STOCKINGS, AND HAS A YULE LOG BURNING BRIGHTLY ON THE HEARTH.

FIRST BROADCAST IN 1966, THE ORIGINAL FILM WORE OUT AFTER JUST FOUR YEARS. THE CURRENT VERSION WAS MADE IN 1970. A SIX-MINUTE SHOT OF FLICKERING FLAMES, IT REPEATS ON AN ENDLESS LOOP, BACKED BY A SOUNDTRACK OF SEASONAL SONGS.

THINKING THAT VIEWERS MIGHT FIND THE FILM OLD-FASHIONED, BROADCASTERS AXED THE YULE LOG SHOW IN 1989. BUT, PERHAPS AS A COMFORTING GESTURE AFTER THE SHOCK OF 9/11, THEY BROUGHT IT BACK FOR CHRISTMAS 2001. TODAY, THE YULE LOG CRACKLES AND SPARKS NOT ONLY ON TV, BUT HAS A WEBSITE AND A PODCAST, AS WELL. IT'S EVEN BEEN REMADE FOR A RIVAL HD CHANNEL — WHERE IT SHOWS FOR 24 HOURS, FROM DAWN ON CHRISTMAS DAY.

Q3

IN CHINA, WHAT GIFTS ARE GIVEN TO FRIENDS AT NEW YEAR AS SYMBOLS OF PLENTY AND GOOD FORTUNE?

a) Little oranges
b) Grapes
c) Biscuits
d) Pears

Q4

TRADITIONALLY IN GERMANY WHAT SHAPE ARE THE CAKES BAKED FOR HERTHA, THE GODDESS OF HEARTH AND HOME?

a) Stockings
b) A fireplace
c) A sleigh
d) Slippers

GET CHASED BY KRAMPUS!

IN AUSTRIA AND THE ALPS, THE KRAMPUS ARE FEARSOME MONSTERS WITH WILD SHAGGY COATS, BIG SHARP TEETH, HUGE LONG HORNS, AND TERRIBLE SHARP CLAWS (THEIR NAME MEANS 'CLAW'). THEY ARE ANCIENT EVIL SPIRITS THAT APPEAR AROUND MIDWINTER. THEY'LL CHASE YOU WITH CHAINS AND BELLS, AND SOME PEOPLE SAY IT'S LUCKY IF THEY CATCH YOU.

Q5

BULGARIA WAS THE LAST COUNTRY TO CONVERT TO THE NEW STYLE OR GREGORIAN CALENDAR, BUT WHEN DID THEY MAKE THE CHANGE?

a) 1925
b) 1954
c) 1960
d) 1968

Q6

IN 2009 WHAT OBJECTS FROM A CHRISTMAS SONG WERE CALCULATED TO COST US $90,000?

a) All the gifts listed in 'The Twelve Days of Christmas'
b) The three ships from 'I Saw Three Ships'
c) The Polar Express train
d) The gold, frankincense and myrrh from 'We Three Kings'

DID YOU KNOW?

THE FIRST MASS OF CHRISTMAS WAS ALWAYS HELD AT THE VERY BEGINNING OF THE DAY: MIDNIGHT! TODAY, MIDNIGHT MASS MARKS THE START OF THE HOLIDAY CELEBRATIONS FOR MILLIONS OF CHRISTIANS — AND FOR MANY, MANY MORE NON-BELIEVERS. THEY GO TO CHURCH TO ENJOY CANDLELIGHT AND CAROLS AND FEEL CLOSE TO THEIR FAMILY. NOW, OVER 2,000 YEARS SINCE JESUS WAS BORN, MIDNIGHT MASS HAS BECOME A CHERISHED MIDWINTER TRADITION.

Q7

WHERE WAS THE ADVENT CALENDAR INVENTED
IN 1851?

a) England
b) France
c) Lapland
d) Germany

Q8

IN WHICH YEAR DID THE SCOTS MAKE CHRISTMAS A
PUBLIC HOLIDAY?

a) 1902
b) 1934
c) 1947
d) 1958

Q9

IN GERMAN-SPEAKING LANDS, IF YOU ARE VISITED BY THE 'STAR-SINGERS,' WHAT WILL THEY SCRIBBLE ABOVE YOUR FRONT DOOR TO BRING YOU GOOD LUCK?

a) Their autographs
b) Your address
c) The date of their visit
d) Their lyrics

Q10

THE FRENCH PHRASE 'AU GUI L'AN NEUF!' (GOOD HEALTH TO THE NEW YEAR!) IS SAID TO BE THE ORIGIN OF THE NAME OF WHICH SCOTTISH CELEBRATION?

a) Candlemas Day
b) Burns Night
c) Michaelmas Day
d) Hogmanay

Q11

WHICH OF THE FOLLOWING IS *NOT* IN THE TOP TEN
NEW YEAR'S RESOLUTIONS ACCORDING TO THE
2010 UNITED STATES GOVERNMENT WEBSITE?

a) Lose weight
b) Take better care of the dog
c) Save money
d) Volunteer to help others

Q12

IN GERMANY, WHO BRINGS PRESENTS ON THE NIGHT
OF CHRISTMAS EVE?

a) Père Noël
b) The Weihnachtsmann
c) Nobody
d) Sooty Peter

Q13

IN GLENLYON, SCOTLAND, WHAT DOES THE LANDLADY GATHER ON A STRAW BRUSH AND SPRINKLE UPON THE WHOLE FAMILY AS THEY ARE GETTING OUT OF BED ON NEW YEAR'S DAY?

a) Urine
b) 'The Cream of the Well' – icy-cold spring water
c) Boiling water
d) Honey

DID YOU KNOW?

ACCORDING TO THE 1990 UNITED STATES GOVERNMENT CENSUS, THE NAME 'CHRISTMAS' AS A SURNAME RANKED 4,757 OUT OF 88,799 DIFFERENT FAMILY NAMES!

Q14

THE CANADIAN POST OFFICE CREATED A SPECIAL ZIP CODE FOR LETTERS TO SANTA IN 1982, BUT WHAT WAS IT?

a) HoH oHo
b) J1N GL3
c) M1NC3 P13
d) S4N T4

Q15

IN PAGAN SCANDINAVIA, WHAT DID PEOPLE TIE TO THE BEDPOST TO BRING THEM SWEET DREAMS?

a) Holly
b) Mistletoe
c) Ivy
d) Stockings

St Thomas's Day – 21 December

In Germany it was said that 'a good meal on St Thomas's Day means you will eat well throughout the year'. A fat pig – your own or a stolen one – was the ideal dinner. And the last student to get out of bed that day was called a 'Lazy Thomas Donkey'.

Q16

In Austria circa 1200, cherry-tree twigs were brought indoors on 4 December, but to celebrate which Saint's day?

a) Saint Christopher
b) Saint Denis
c) Saint Barbara
d) Saint Elmo

Q17

WHAT WAS 'ANGELS' HAIR', INVENTED IN GERMANY IN 1610?

a) Paper chains
b) Tinsel
c) A sweet
d) A Christmas song

Q18

WHAT WAS FIRST MADE IN FRANCE IN 1820 FROM HOLLOW GLASS, WATER AND CHIPS OF BONE?

a) A bubble light
b) Angel chimes
c) Baubles
d) A snow-globe

Q19

DURING WHICH DECADE WAS THE FIRST IN-STORE
SANTA CLAUS INTRODUCED TO MACY'S IN
NEW YORK?

a) 1870s
b) 1900s
c) 1920s
d) 1940s

Q20

IN 1882 EDWARD H. JOHNSON, OF EDISON
ELECTRIC LIGHT COMPANY, USA, WAS THE FIRST
TO DECORATE HIS TREE WITH ELECTRIC LIGHT
BULBS, BUT WHAT COLOUR WERE THE LIGHTS?

a) Green and red
b) White
c) Red and gold
d) Red, white and blue

BEWARE THE CHRISTMAS CAT...

IN NORTHERN EUROPE IT WAS MOST UNLUCKY TO LEAVE WORK — SUCH AS SPINNING THREAD OR SEWING CLOTHES — UNFINISHED AT CHRISTMAS. IN ICELAND, FARMERS TRADITIONALLY GAVE NEW GARMENTS TO THEIR WORKERS THEN, AND PARENTS GAVE CLOTHES TO THEIR CHILDREN. IF THEY HAD NOT GOT THESE READY BY 23 DECEMBER, THE CHRISTMAS CAT — OR A FRIGHTFUL GOBLIN CALLED TORLAK — WOULD COME TO GET THEM!

Q21

BETWEEN 2003 AND 2007 HOW MANY DEATHS, ON AVERAGE, WERE CAUSED PER YEAR BY CHRISTMAS TREE FIRES IN THE USA?

a) 0
b) 6
c) 14
d) 35

CHRISTMAS TRADITIONS

Q22

WHICH WORD, DESCRIBING WHEN THE TOP AND
BOTTOM OF THE TILTING EARTH GETS CLOSEST TO,
OR FURTHEST AWAY FROM THE SUN, COMES FROM
TWO EXISTING LATIN WORDS MEANING 'THE SUN'
AND 'TO STAY STILL'?

a) Sunstay
b) Solstice
c) Soltere
d) Sunstill

Q23

WHAT WAS THE NAME OF THE ANCIENT ROMAN GOD
OF SEEDS AND FERTILITY?

a) Venus
b) Jupiter
c) Pluto
d) Saturn

WHEN CHRISTMAS WAS BANNED...

IN 1644, PURITANS RULED ENGLAND, WALES, SCOTLAND AND IRELAND. THEY THOUGHT THAT OLD CHRISTMAS TRADITIONS WERE WRONG, AND FORBADE THEM. FOR 16 YEARS, UNTIL THE PURITAN GOVERNMENT WAS REPLACED BY CATHOLIC KING CHARLES II IN 1660, CHRISTMAS CELEBRATIONS WERE FORBIDDEN.

Q24

HOW DID ROMAN WRITER PLINY THE YOUNGER (AD C. 62 – 113) HIDE AWAY FROM THE SATURNALIA PARTY?

a) He had a special soundproof room built.
b) He left the country.
c) He moved into a woodland hideout.
d) He sedated himself for a week.

Q25

WHAT IS THE NAME OF THE ANCIENT MIDWINTER TRADITION, A RELIC OF SCANDINAVIAN CUSTOMS, THAT WASHINGTON IRVING WROTE ABOUT IN 1820?

a) The Yule Goat
b) Christmas Ham
c) The Yule Clog
d) Carol singing

 AT CHRISTMAS PLAY AND MAKE GOOD CHEER, FOR CHRISTMAS COMES BUT ONCE A YEAR.

ENGLISH POET AND FARMER
THOMAS TUSSER (c.1524–1580)

Q26

WHO ARE THE AUTHORS OF THE FOUR GOSPELS?

a) Peter, Paul, Simon and James
b) Luke, Richard, Neil and Mark
c) Matthew, Mark, Luke and John
d) John, James, Mark and Tim

Q27

WHICH OF THE FOLLOWING IS THE HIGHEST RANK OF ANGELS?

a) Cherubim
b) Archangels
c) Dominions
d) Virtues

Q28

'GOD REST YOU MERRY, GENTLEMEN, LET NOTHING YOU DISMAY.' WHEN WERE THE WORDS OF THIS CAROL WRITTEN?

a) AD 1770
b) AD 354
c) 1876
d) 1999

RING OUT, WILD BELLS

RING OUT, WILD BELLS, TO THE WILD SKY,
THE FLYING CLOUD, THE FROSTY NIGHT:
THE YEAR IS DYING IN THE NIGHT,
RING OUT, WILD BELLS, AND LET HIM DIE.

RING OUT THE OLD, RING IN THE NEW,
RING, HAPPY BELLS, ACROSS THE SNOW:
THE YEAR IS GOING, LET HIM GO;
RING OUT THE FALSE, RING IN THE TRUE...

ALFRED LORD TENNYSON (1809–1892)

Q29

WHEN DID EARLY CHRISTIAN THEOLOGIAN HIPPOLYTUS OF ROME CELEBRATE CHRISTMAS DAY?

a) 25 December
b) 1 January
c) 2 April
d) 21 June

Q30

WHICH WESTERN CHURCH SERVICE TAKES IT NAME FROM ITS CLOSING WORDS, 'GO! IT IS FINISHED'?

a) Evensong
b) Easter Vigil
c) Compline
d) Mass

Q31

WHERE DOES THE WORD 'XMAS' ORIGINATE FROM?

a) It is a modern invention to avoid using the religious name 'Christ' at a multicultural holiday.

b) It is early Greek code – the X represents a holy symbol for the very first Christians.

c) It is a lazy, disrespectful way of writing 'Christmas'.

d) It comes from texting shorthand.

DID YOU KNOW?

IN BRITAIN YOU SHOULD EAT A MINCE PIE AT A DIFFERENT HOUSE ON EACH OF THE TWELVE DAYS OF CHRISTMAS. IT'S MEANT TO BRING GOOD LUCK FOR EVERY MONTH OF THE YEAR.

Q32

WHICH OF THE FOLLOWING WAS BELIEVED TO BE
TRUE OF ANY CHILD BORN ON CHRISTMAS DAY?

a) They will never see – or be frightened by
   – a ghost.
b) They will never be drowned or hanged.
c) There is a danger that they might turn into
   a werewolf.
d) All of the above.

Q33

ACCORDING TO A POEM WRITTEN AROUND 1525,
WHAT WILL HAPPEN TO A BABY BORN ON CHRISTMAS
DAY IF CHRISTMAS IS ON A SATURDAY?

a) In six months he will die.
b) He will be a great lord.
c) He will be brave and cheery.
d) He will be greedy.

Q34

WHO SOLVED THE DATING DILEMMA BY CREATING
LISTS OF YEARS BASED ON THE DATE THAT JESUS
CHRIST WAS CONCEIVED?

a) Dennis the Tall
b) Roger the Tidy
c) Dennis the Small
d) Roger the Hairy

Q35

WHAT DOES AD STAND FOR WHEN REFERRING
TO DATES?

a) Access Denied
b) After Date
c) Anno Domini
d) Alternate Date

Q36

WHAT IS THE NAME OF A CANDLE STUCK INTO AN ORANGE, DECORATED WITH DRIED FRUITS AND WRAPPED WITH A RED RIBBON?

a) A Ribbon Orange
b) A Christingle
c) The Orange Light
d) A Candle Fruit

THE NUTCRACKER

A FAMOUS CHRISTMAS ENTERTAINMENT, TCHAIKOVSKY'S BALLET THE NUTCRACKER (FIRST PERFORMED IN RUSSIA IN 1892), TELLS THE STORY OF A CHILD'S MAGIC JOURNEY TO THE KINGDOM OF SWEETS, WHERE SHE IS GREETED BY THE SUGARPLUM FAIRY!

FEELING HUNGRY?

LIKE THE SOUTHERN FRENCH, INDULGE YOURSELF IN THE 'THIRTEEN DESSERTS'. THIS BUFFET COMMEMORATES THE TWELVE HOLY APOSTLES – JESUS'S FRIENDS AND FOLLOWERS – PLUS BABY JESUS.

ALMONDS
WALNUTS
RAISINS
FIGS OR DATES
APPLES AND PEARS
ORANGES OR TANGERINES
GRAPES OR WINTER MELON
QUINCE PASTE AND CANDIED FRUITS
PALE NOUGAT
DARK NOUGAT
CAKES AND COOKIES
CALISSONS (SOFT ALMOND SWEETS)
FOUGASSE (SWEET SPICED BREAD)

Q37

WHAT IS BLACK TOM OF SOOTHILL?

a) A 700-year-old bell.
b) A gun fired to scare evil spirits away.
c) The largest Yule Log on record.
d) A Christmas cat that would chase after people who had not got their presents ready by 23 December.

Q38

WHICH OF THESE SHOULD YOU BE WARY OF DOING ON 28 DECEMBER, A TRADITIONALLY UNLUCKY DAY?

a) Cutting your nails
b) All of the answers
c) Beginning a new project
d) Putting on new clothes

RUDOLPH THE RED-NOSED REINDEER

THIS STORY WAS WRITTEN IN 1939 BY ROBERT L. MAY IN THE USA AND BECAME A WORLDWIDE HIT. IT TELLS THE TALE OF SANTA CLAUS'S NINTH AND LEAD REINDEER WHO POSSESSES AN UNUSUALLY RED NOSE THAT GIVES OFF ITS OWN LIGHT, POWERFUL ENOUGH TO ILLUMINATE THE TEAM'S PATH THROUGH THE WINTER WEATHER. THE SONG OF THE SAME TITLE DATES FROM 1949.

Q39

IN BRITAIN, IT IS SUPPOSED TO BE UNLUCKY TO LEAVE CHRISTMAS DECORATIONS UP AFTER WHAT DATE?

a) 1 January
b) 3 January
c) 6 January
d) 9 January

Q40

WHAT IS THE NAME OF THE GAME PLAYED IN NORTH LINCOLNSHIRE TO COMMEMORATE THE LOVELY LADY OF THE MANOR, WHOSE HOOD BLEW OFF IN THE WINTER WIND?

a) The Lincolnshire Hood Race
b) The Lady's Hat Game
c) The Boggins' Hood Chase
d) The Haxey Hood Game

Q41

WHO WROTE THE POEM 'A VISIT FROM ST NICHOLAS' — WHICH BEGINS WITH THE LINE ''TWAS THE NIGHT BEFORE CHRISTMAS', IN 1823?

a) Rev J. H. Hopkins Jnr
b) Robert Herrick
c) The Grimm brothers
d) Clement Clarke Moore

Q42

WHAT HAPPENED CIRCA 1890 WHICH CREATED A
PROBLEM FOR MANY NATIONAL POST OFFICES?

a) There was a postal workers' strike.
b) There was a mass shortage of postage
stamps.
c) Children started posting letters to Santa
Claus.
d) A huge snowstorm meant that many letters
were misplaced.

Q43

IN 2007, HOW MUCH WAS 'THE AVERAGE PERSON' IN
THE UK SAID TO SPEND ON CHRISTMAS GIFTS?

a) £150
b) £384
c) £501
d) £279

Q44

WHAT ROYAL NAMES WERE GIVEN TO THE THREE KINGS AROUND AD 500?

a) Stretch, Fatso and Stinkie
b) Athos, Porthos and Aramis
c) Caspar, Melchior and Balthasar
d) Matthew, Mark and Luke

AT CHRISTMAS BE MERYE, AND THANKFUL WITHAL
AND FEAST THY POORE NEIGHBOURS YE GRET WITH YE SMALL...

POET THOMAS TUSSER, ENGLAND (c.1550)

'THE DRUIDS . . . HOLD NOTHING MORE SACRED THAN MISTLETOE . . . WHEN THEY DISCOVER SOME, GROWING ON AN OAK TREE, THEY GATHER IT WITH GREAT CEREMONY ON THE NINTH DAY OF THE MOON. . . THEY PRAISE THE MOON, CALLING IT 'HEALER OF ALL', THEN PREPARE A RITUAL SACRIFICE AND FEAST . . . THEY BRING TWO WHITE BULLS . . . A PRIEST DRESSED IN WHITE ROBES CLIMBS THE TREE AND CUTS DOWN THE MISTLETOE, USING A GOLDEN SICKLE. ONLOOKERS CATCH IT AS IT FALLS, IN A WHITE CLOAK. THEN THE BULLS ARE SACRIFICED . . .'

ROMAN WRITER PLINY THE YOUNGER (AD 62–113)

Q45

WHICH PLANT HAS PREVIOUSLY BEEN KNOWN AS 'CUETLAXOCHITL' (SKIN-FLOWER) AND 'NOCHE BUENA' (THE FLOWER OF CHRISTMAS EVE)?

a) Ivy
b) Poinsettia
c) Mexican Marigold
d) Mistletoe

Q46

WHERE DID PANTOMIME ORIGINATE?

a) Ancient Egypt
b) Ancient Rome
c) Ancient Greece
d) Victorian times

Q47

WHICH 'SQUEEZING, WRENCHING, GRASPING, SCRAPING, CLUTCHING, COVETOUS, OLD SINNER' IS FAMOUSLY VISITED BY GHOSTS ON CHRISTMAS EVE?

a) Ebenezer Scrooge
b) Queen Victoria
c) Charles Dickens
d) Washington Irving

Q48

WHY DID ROBINS START APPEARING ON CHRISTMAS CARDS SOON AFTER THEY WERE INVENTED IN 1843?

a) Because the man who sent the first Christmas card was named Robin.
b) Because robins were used to deliver the cards around the country.
c) Because robins can only be seen on Christmas Day.
d) Because robins reminded Victorians of the red jackets of the postal workers who delivered their cards.

DID YOU KNOW...?

SANTA'S WIFE FIRST APPEARS IN PRINT IN 1889 IN A POEM BY AMERICAN KATHERINE L. BATES, 'GOODY SANTA CLAUS ON A SLEIGH RIDE'.

BAH! HUMBUG!... EVERY IDIOT WHO GOES ABOUT WITH 'MERRY CHRISTMAS' ON HIS LIPS, SHOULD BE BOILED WITH HIS OWN PUDDING, AND BURIED WITH A STAKE OF HOLLY THROUGH HIS HEART.

EBENEZER SCROOGE, IN CHARLES DICKENS'S' STORY *A CHRISTMAS CAROL* (1843)

EXTRA
HELPINGS

Q49

EARLY CHRISTIANS CALLED THE DAYS LEADING UP TO CHRISTMAS 'ADVENT'. THE DAYS WERE OFTEN GLOOMY AND SORROWFUL AND GANGS OF TEENAGERS ROAMED THE STREETS, 'BOUNCING AND BEATING ON EVERY DOOR'. BUT WHAT COULD YOU OFFER THEM TO GET RID OF THEM?

a) Beer
b) Dried fruit
c) Meat
d) An orange

Q50

WHICH OF THE FOLLOWING IS NOT A NAME FOR A FESTIVE FEAST?

a) Sowans
b) Julbord
c) Le Réveillon
d) Drei Königs Tag

Q51

WHAT COULD THE ACT OF PLACING MARKED ONIONS IN A WARM PLACE AND WAITING FOR ONE TO SPROUT GREEN SHOOTS REVEAL, ACCORDING TO AN OLD MAGIC SPELL?

a) A young girl's future husband.
b) A young boy's future height.
c) Whether or not it will be a white Christmas.
d) Whether a pregnant woman's baby will be a boy or a girl.

HEAP ON MORE WOOD! THE WIND IS CHILL;
BUT LET IT WHISTLE AS IT WILL,
WE'LL KEEP OUR CHRISTMAS MERRY STILL.

SCOTTISH NOVELIST AND POET SIR WALTER SCOTT (1771–1832)

DID YOU KNOW?

CHRISTMAS ROSES, WHICH BLOOM AT MIDWINTER, ARE SO POISONOUS (THEY CAUSE TERRIBLE DIARRHOEA) THAT THEY WERE USED AS A CHEMICAL WEAPON BY ANCIENT GREEK ARMIES.

Q52

OVER THE CHRISTMAS SEASON OF 1289, HOW MANY DOVES DID ONE ENGLISH NOBLE AND HIS 70 GUESTS EAT?

a) 1
b) 28
c) 71
d) 4

Q53

IN RUSSIAN TRADITION WHAT MUST YOU THROW AT THE CEILING TO FORETELL WHETHER BEES WILL GIVE LOTS OF HONEY NEXT YEAR (IF IT STICKS, THEY WILL)?

a) Pickled herring
b) Stewed eels
c) Pale nougat
d) Porridge

'HOUSE-BLING'

IN 2004, A HOME COVERED IN 20,000 LIGHTS CAUSED TRAFFIC DISRUPTION, COMPLAINTS FROM NEIGHBOURS, INCREASED CRIME - AND COST OVER £7,000 TO POLICE.

Q54

WHAT IS THE NAME OF THE PEASANT DISH MADE BY SOAKING WHOLE WHEAT GRAINS IN WATER OVERNIGHT AND THEN SIMMERING THEM IN MILK FOR HOURS AND HOURS?

a) Flummery
b) Frumenty
c) Scrapple
d) Brown Betty

KISSING UNDER THE MISTLETOE WAS A PECULIARLY ENGLISH TRADITION. BUT ON NEW YEAR'S EVE IN AUSTRIA, THERE WAS A SIMILAR CUSTOM. A MYSTERIOUS MASKED FIGURE, AN UGLY OLD MAN, SAT UNDER A PINE-TREE BRANCH IN DARK CORNERS OF COUNTRY INNS. HE WORE A WREATH OF MISTLETOE. WHEN A PRETTY GIRL PASSED, HE JUMPED UP 'AND IMPRINTED A ROUGH KISS'. WHEN MIDNIGHT STRUCK, HE WAS DRIVEN OUT INTO THE SNOW TO DIE (OR PRETEND TO), AS A SYMBOL OF THE OLD YEAR.

FROM STAGE TO SITTING ROOM

RELIGIOUS PLAYS — SOMETIMES CALLED MYSTERY PLAYS — BRING BIBLE STORIES TO LIFE IN TOWN STREETS AND IN CHURCHES. STAGED ON 24 DECEMBER, THEY CELEBRATE THE FEAST OF ADAM AND EVE. TO REPRESENT THE TREE IN PARADISE FROM WHICH EVE TOOK THE APPLE OF KNOWLEDGE, PERFORMERS USE AN EVERGREEN HUNG WITH APPLES AND OTHER DECORATIONS, BECAUSE REAL APPLE-TREE BRANCHES ARE BARE IN DECEMBER.

Q55

WHAT IS THE SCOTTISH EQUIVALENT TO PLUM PUDDING — LATER CALLED CHRISTMAS PUDDING — WHICH IS EATEN AT NEW YEAR, NOT CHRISTMAS, AND COVERED IN THICK PASTRY?

a) Scotch pie
b) Clanger
c) Black bun
d) Squab pie

Q56

WHERE DO TURKEYS COME FROM?

a) America
b) Turkey
c) Wales
d) Australia

Q57

WHEN DID COCA-COLA START THEIR SERIES OF
CHRISTMAS ADVERTISEMENTS FEATURING A SMILING,
COLA-DRINKING SANTA CLAUS?

a) 1931
b) 1939
c) 1946
d) 1947

INSTANT TRADITION

1880, TRURO, SOUTHWEST ENGLAND: IN A WOODEN SHED, THE LOCAL BISHOP HELD THE FIRST-EVER SERVICE OF NINE LESSONS [BIBLE READINGS] AND CAROLS. IN 1918, HIS IDEA WAS COPIED AT KING'S COLLEGE, CAMBRIDGE, HOME OF A WORLD-FAMOUS CHOIR. THE SERVICE WAS FIRST BROADCAST IN 1928 AND HAS BEEN EVER SINCE, EXCEPT FOR JUST ONE YEAR (1930).

1742, DUBLIN, IRELAND: FIRST PERFORMANCE OF GERMAN-BORN, LONDON-RESIDENT, G. F. HANDEL'S MESSIAH: 'A SORT OF 18TH-CENTURY MUSICAL' ORIGINALLY WRITTEN FOR EASTER. BY THE MID-1800S IT HAD BECOME VASTLY POPULAR, WITH PRE-CHRISTMAS RECITALS BY MASSED CHOIRS AND ORCHESTRAS OF OVER 3,000 PERFORMERS ATTRACTING AUDIENCES OF 10,000 AND MORE.

Q58

WHY SHOULD YOU NOT EAT MISTLETOE BERRIES?

a) They taste disgusting.
b) It will bring bad luck.
c) Mistletoe doesn't have berries.
d) They are very poisonous.

STRANGE BUT TRUE

SEVEN OUT OF EVERY TEN BRITISH DOGS ARE GIVEN CHRISTMAS PRESENTS.

FOOTPRINTS FROM THE FUTURE

IF YOU'RE FEELING BRAVE, YOU MIGHT LIKE TO TRY THIS ANCIENT NEW YEAR'S EVE CUSTOM:

LATE AT NIGHT, SPREAD ASHES SMOOTHLY ON THE HEARTH.

BY MORNING, YOU SHOULD FIND A FOOTPRINT IN THEM.

IF IT POINTS TOWARDS THE DOOR, A FAMILY MEMBER WILL DIE. IF IT POINTS INWARDS, THERE WILL BE A NEW BABY!

DID YOU KNOW?

BRITONS THROW AWAY AROUND 83 SQUARE MILES OF WRAPPING PAPER EACH CHRISTMAS.

Q59

WHAT TIME DID QUEEN VICTORIA'S CHRISTMAS DINNER BEGIN?

a) 10 am
b) 3 pm
c) 9 pm
d) 11 pm

Q60

OVER CHRISTMAS 2008, EACH BRITISH PERSON ATE, ON AVERAGE, 27 OF WHAT?

a) Brussels sprouts
b) Mince pies
c) Roast potatoes
d) Gingerbread men

LET'S GO MUMPING!

ST THOMAS'S DAY, 21 DECEMBER, WAS THE THIRD TIME IN ADVENT WHEN RICH FAMILIES IN ENGLAND WERE EXPECTED TO GIVE GENEROUSLY TO THE POOR. CHILDREN SMEARED THEIR FACES WITH SOOT AND WENT 'A-THOMASING' OR 'A-MUMPING', TO BEG FOR MONEY. FROM ST THOMAS'S DAY TO TWELFTH NIGHT, TROOPS OF GUISERS OR MUMMERS — ALL MEN — ALSO DEMANDED PAYMENT. DRESSED IN MASKS WITH ANIMAL HEADS, OR HIDDEN UNDER TATTERED, RAGGED COSTUMES, THEY DANCED AND SANG, PERFORMED AN ANCIENT PLAY — AND PROBABLY USED THEIR DISGUISES AS COVER WHILE COMMITTING SERIOUS CRIMES. IN THE 16TH CENTURY, KING HENRY VIII MADE WEARING MASKS A CRIME, PUNISHABLE BY THREE MONTHS IN PRISON.

Q61

IN ICELAND, WHAT CREATURE DID PEOPLE
TRADITIONALLY SWEAR OATHS OVER AT CHRISTMAS?

a) A boar
b) A goat
c) A shark
d) A horse

Q62

WHY IS IT TECHNICALLY STILL ILLEGAL TO EAT A
MINCE PIE ON CHRISTMAS DAY IN BRITAIN?

a) Because of a spate of deaths caused by
   overeating in the 18th century.
b) Because King James I banned them after a
   would-be assassin tried to poison him with
   one, and the law has never been changed.
c) Because Oliver Cromwell banned them
   when he ruled Britain and the law has never
   been changed.
d) It isn't. This is a festive trick question.

Q63

KING HENRY VIII BANNED THE PLAYING OF ALL
SPORTS ON CHRISTMAS DAY, APART FROM ONE.
WHAT WAS IT?

a) Badminton
b) Croquet
c) Competitive sprinting
d) Archery

Q64

WHAT IS THE TOTAL NUMBER OF PRESENTS GIVEN
AWAY IN THE CHRISTMAS CAROL 'THE TWELVE DAYS
OF CHRISTMAS'?

a) 532
b) 364
c) 450
d) 238

❝ WE ATTENDED DIVINE SERVICE IN THE CHAPEL OF PRAHIA (NEW ZEALAND); PART OF THE SERVICE BEING READ IN ENGLISH, AND PART IN THE NATIVE LANGUAGE... WE DID NOT HEAR OF ANY RECENT ACTS OF CANNIBALISM; BUT MR STOKES FOUND BURNT HUMAN BONES STREWED ROUND A FIRE-PLACE ON A SMALL ISLAND... **❞**

CHARLES DARWIN, *BEAGLE* DIARIES (1835)

Q65

WHAT WAS INTERESTING ABOUT THE UK CHRISTMAS NUMBER ONE SONG, THE FLYING PICKETS' COVER VERSION OF YAZOO'S 'ONLY YOU'?

a) It was performed without instruments.
b) It was performed only on the triangle.
c) It was performed for the Pope on Christmas Day.
d) It was performed without lyrics.

Q66

HOW MANY TREES HAVE TO BE CHOPPED DOWN TO PRODUCE THE 1.8 BILLION CHRISTMAS CARDS BRITONS SEND EACH CHRISTMAS?

a) 10,000
b) 20,000
c) 100,000
d) 200,000

Q67

WHICH ELEMENT OF SANTA CLAUS WAS INVENTED BY DRINKS MANUFACTURER THE COCA COLA COMPANY?

a) His white beard
b) His red suit
c) His sleigh
d) None of the above

Q68

ACCORDING TO THE HOLY DAYS AND FASTING DAYS ACT OF 1551, WHAT MUST YOU NOT DO ON YOUR WAY TO MASS?

a) Travel by horse
b) Wear any gold
c) Talk to anyone
d) Hop and skip

Q69

IN JAPAN, WHAT IS IT INADVISABLE TO GIVE SOMEONE AT CHRISTMAS?

a) Confectionery in a plastic wrapping
b) A Christmas card in a red envelope
c) Black socks
d) Anything with 'Xmas' written on it.

Q70

WHICH IS THE ONLY COUNTRY IN EASTERN ASIA TO RECOGNISE CHRISTMAS WITH A NATIONAL HOLIDAY?

a) Malaysia
b) South Korea
c) Japan
d) North Korea

Q71

IN UKRAINE, WHAT IS SAID TO BRING GOOD LUCK IF SEEN ON CHRISTMAS MORNING?

a) A crow perched on a snowman
b) A fly in your drink
c) A crack in the wall
d) A spider web

Q72

WHAT WAS CHARLES DICKENS'S INITIAL CHOICE FOR SCROOGE'S EXCLAMATION 'BAH! HUMBUG!' IN *A CHRISTMAS CAROL*?

a) 'Bah! Tidings!'
b) 'Bah! Yule!'
c) 'Bah! Christmas!'
d) 'Bah! Holiday!'

ONE VERY SPECIAL CHRISTMAS

BETWEEN 1914 AND 1918, EUROPEAN NATIONS AND THEIR ALLIES WORLDWIDE FOUGHT 'THE WAR TO END ALL WARS'. IT BROUGHT DEATH AND SUFFERING ON A NEW AND TERRIBLE SCALE. BUT, EVEN IN THE MIDDLE OF APPALLING BLOODSHED, CHRISTMAS TIME PROMISED PEACE, FOR A WHILE, TO SOLDIERS ON BOTH SIDES. BRIEF CHRISTMAS TRUCES WERE ARRANGED; THE MOST FAMOUS WAS IN 1914, WHEN ALLIED AND GERMAN TROOPS EXCHANGED GIFTS OF FOOD AND SOUVENIRS, AND SANG CAROLS TO EACH OTHER. THEY WERE ORDERED TO START KILLING AGAIN AT NEW YEAR.

ANSWERS

CHRISTMAS AROUND THE WORLD

Q1: B. THEY FEASTED ON A PIG

Orkney was settled by Vikings from Scandinavia around AD 900.

Q2: B. THREE TIMES

In the Balkans they wrap their log in silk and offer it wine!

Q3: A. LITTLE ORANGES

In Europe and North America, little oranges are a fruity treat often tucked into the toes of children's Christmas stockings.

Q4: D. SLIPPERS

Germans also roll huge blazing wheels downhill to encourage the midwinter sun.

Q5: D. 1968

England did not change its calendar until 1752, when an Act of Parliament ordered that Old 2 September must be followed by New 13 September.

Q6: A. THE TWELVE DAYS OF CHRISTMAS

The first known English version of these words dates from around AD 1250, but they were probably composed even earlier, in France. Originally the song was a memory game.

Q7: D. GERMANY

Before this, pious families hung up little holy pictures, day by day, or marked time from 1 until 24 December by chalking a line on the wall.

Q8: D. 1958

Traditionally in Scotland on Christmas day people eat 'care-cakes' in bed, baked in honour of the Virgin Mary.

Q9: C. THE DATE OF THEIR VISIT

They will be dressed as the Wise Men plus their guiding star.

Q10: D. HOGMANAY

In Iceland, people believe that the cows start to talk and seals transform themselves into humans on New Year's Eve!

Q11: B. TAKE BETTER CARE OF THE DOG

Some of the other top resolutions include getting a better job, taking a trip and stopping smoking.

Q12: B. THE WEIHNACHTSMANN

Sooty Peter does actually sometimes accompany St Nicholas in the Netherlands, but he is a scary friend and helper.

Q13: A. URINE

This was a good-luck ceremony designed to keep witches away, recorded in 1888.

Q14: A. HoH oHO

The USA and Canada created NORAD in 1958 to keep watch for airborne invaders. At Christmas time, it also claims to track Santa's flight from the North Pole.

Q15: A. HOLLY

Holly gave a home to wandering winter spirits and its sharp spikes, hung at doors and windows, also kept them (and other evil-doers) safely out of the house.

Q16: C. SAINT BARBARA

If kept in a warm place, they will bloom at Christmas.

Q17: B. TINSEL

At first it was made of real silver foil, cut into long thin strips. Later, it was made from (poisonous) lead or pewter. It was originally used to drape holy statues.

Q18: D. A SNOW-GLOBE

Soon after these were invented, maths masters at a religious school in Germany accidentally invented a new Christmas decoration, the 'Moravian Star', by making paper models to help pupils understand geometry.

Q19: A. 1870s

Macy's also pioneered special Christmas window displays.

Q20: D. RED, WHITE AND BLUE

Electric lights were first used on outdoor trees in the USA in 1956!

Q21: C. 14

Fire-fighters were called out to around 250 Christmas tree fires every year.

CHRISTMAS IS FORCED UPON A RELUCTANT AND DISGUSTED NATION BY THE SHOPKEEPERS AND THE PRESS; ON ITS OWN MERITS IT WOULD WITHER AND SHRIVEL IN THE FIERY BREATH OF UNIVERSAL HATRED.

ANGLO-IRISH DRAMATIST AND ACTIVIST GEORGE BERNARD SHAW (1856–1950)

CHRISTMAS
TRADITIONS

Q22: B. SOLSTICE

These moments happen at the longest (Midsummer) and shortest (Midwinter) days.

Q23: D. SATURN

In mid-southern Italy, the weeks after the winter solstice were a good time to start clearing fields and planting crops. They asked Saturn to help them by offering human sacrifices.

Q24: A. HE HAD A SOUNDPROOF ROOM

The festival eventually lasted a week, unti 24 December.

Q25: C. THE YULE CLOG

He described it as 'a great log of wood, sometimes the root of a tree, brought into the house with great ceremony...laid in the fireplace, and lighted with the brand of last year's clog'.

Q26: C. MATTHEW, MARK, LUKE AND JOHN

Only Matthew and Luke tell of the birth of Jesus.

Q27: A. CHERUBIM

Beware of the fallen, rebellious angel Lucifer!

Q28: A. AD 1770

The carol is referred to in Charles Dickens's *A Christmas Carol* from 1843.

Q29: C. 2 APRIL

Clement of Alexandria celebrated Christmas on 18 November or 20 May!

Q30: D. MASS

In England, the earliest recorded use of the day-name 'Christes Maesse' is dated 1038, making it one of the oldest words in the English language.

Q31: B. EARLY GREEK CODE

The early printers' shorthand version of 'Xtian' = 'Christian' has not been so widely copied.

Q32: D. ALL OF THE ABOVE

It is also believed that they will always be lucky.

Q33: A. IN SIX MONTHS HE WILL DIE

If born on a Friday he will be long-lived and loving.

Q34: C. DENNIS THE SMALL (DIONYSIUS EXIGUUS)

Unlike Christmas, Easter Day is not fixed, but depends on the phases of the moon.

Q35: C. ANNO DOMINI (IN THE YEAR OF OUR LORD)

The dates count forward to the present moment from AD 1, and backwards into the distant past from 1 BC. There is no year 0 (zero) between them.

Q36: B. A CHRISTINGLE

These were first handed out to Czech children in Advent 1747 to remind them that Jesus is 'the Light of the World'.

Q37: A. A 700-YEAR-OLD BELL

The bell in Dewsbury, West Yorkshire, is rung once for each year since Jesus was born, ending at midnight on Christmas Eve.

Q38: B. ALL OF THE ANSWERS

In Spain, people will play practical jokes on you and try and make you believe the most absurd stories. If you fall for their tricks, they'll call you 'innocente!' which means 'fool' as well as 'young child.'

Q39: C. 6 JANUARY

According to tradition the decorations must be burnt, fed to the cattle or buried!

Q40: D. THE HAXEY HOOD GAME

Teams of 'boggins' (men from rival villages) still fight to get hold of a 'hood' (rope wrapped in leather) and carry it back to their local public house. This can take several hours.

Q41: D. CLEMENT CLARKE MOORE

The poem is largely credited for the contemporary Christmas lore of the eight flying reindeer and their names: Dasher, Dancer, Prancer, Vixen, Comet, Cupid, Donner and Blitzen.

Q42: C. CHILDREN POSTED LETTERS TO SANTA

This was also around the time that the first actor was hired to impersonate Santa Claus in a US department store.

Q43: B. £384

In 2009, 45% of British adults worried about spending too much money at Christmas.

Q44: C. CASPAR, MELCHIOR AND BALTHAZAR

Caspar was young, and from the Mediterranean or maybe Europe. Melchior was old, and from Arabia or Asia. Balthazar was middle-aged and African.

Q45: B. POINSETTIA

The ancient Aztecs of Mexico used the bright red and green poinsettia plant to dye cloth, and as a medicine.

Q46: C. ANCIENT GREECE

In the modern tradition, 'Principal Boys' are always played by attractive young women and 'Pantomime Dames' are always acted by comic old men.

Q47: A. EBENEZER SCROOGE

Written in 1843, *A Christmas Carol* quickly became the world's best-known Christmas story.

Q48: D. RED JACKETS OF THE POSTAL WORKERS

The first Christmas card depicted a happy Victorian family feasting and also handing out food and clothes to beggars.

THE WAR ON CHRISTMAS: HOW THE LIBERAL PLOT TO BAN THE SACRED CHRISTIAN HOLIDAY IS WORSE THAN YOU THOUGHT

BOOK TITLE, USA, 2007

EACH NATION, NATURALLY, HAS
FASHIONED ITS OWN CHRISTMAS.
THE ENGLISH HAVE MADE IT A
SEASON OF SOLID COMFORT, OF
GOOD FELLOWSHIP AND 'CHARITY',
WITH A SLIGHT FLAVOUR OF
SOOTHING RELIGION...

BRITISH HISTORIAN CLEMENT A. MILES, 1912

EXTRA

HELPINGS

Q49: B. DRIED FRUIT

Thursdays were the most gloomy days because 'dreadful devils' escaped from Hell to tempt Christian men and women.

Q50: A. SOWANS

Sowans is actually a Scottish dish made from the outer chaff of oat-grains, soaked and boiled until it's brown and sticky like treacle. Somehow, it tastes both sickly-sweet and sour.

Q51: A. A YOUNG GIRL'S FUTURE HUSBAND

The girls could also try going to the pigsty late one night and calling to the pigs. If a big pig grunts first, you'll marry an old man; if it's a small one, you'll wed a young one!

Q52: D. 4

They also ate 1 boar, the best part of 3 bullocks, 2 young calves, 4 pigs, 60 chickens, 8 partridges plus bread and cheese!

Q53: D. PORRIDGE

The Russian-style porridge is called 'kutya' and its plump grains are a sign of hope and new life, even in winter. Add honey for happiness and success, and poppy seeds for a peaceful rest.

Q54: B. FRUMENTY

If peasants could afford it, they would add cinnamon, a few raisins or honey.

Q55: C. BLACK BUN

The cake mixture typically contains raisins, currants, almonds, citrus peel, allspice, ginger, cinnamon and pepper. Although the meat and onions from earlier recipes are today left out, some do still include suet and carrots.

Q56: A. AMERICA

King Henry VIII was Britain's first royal turkey eater, as such exotic rarities could only be enjoyed by the super-rich.

Q57: A. 1931

Contrary to urban legend, they did not change the colour of his costume to match the labels on their bottles. It had been red since the 1860s.

Q58: D. THEY ARE VERY POISONOUS

According to Viking myths, Freya, goddess of love, ordered that mistletoe should grow half-way between earth and sky. When people walked under trees where it grew, they kissed, to please her.

Q59: C. 9 pm

In the 1830s they ate goose or beef, but by around 1900, turkey was the favourite.

Q60: B. MINCE PIES

On average, each British person gains 2 kg over the Christmas holidays!

Q61: A. A BOAR

Families would join hands and make a solemn promise, then sacrifice the poor creature. Yule was the traditional time for swearing oaths.

Q62: C. BECAUSE OLIVER CROMWELL BANNED THEM

Oliver Cromwell was a Puritan, and so all unnecessary festivities and enjoyment were severely frowned upon. Sports were banned and theatres were shut down too.

Q63: D. ARCHERY

In 1541, Henry VIII introduced the Unlawful Games Act, which banned the playing of all sports on Christmas Day apart from archery, which was seen as essential to maintaining the country's military strength.

Q64: B. 364

The twelve days in the song are the twelve days from Christmas Day to the day before Epiphany, 5 January.

Q65: A. IT WAS PERFORMED WITHOUT INSTRUMENTS

The song was formed completely *a cappella* (without accompaniment) and hit the top spot in 1983.

Q66: D. 200,000

Thankfully, many greetings-card manufacturers operate a policy of planting new trees wherever they fell them.

Q67: D. NONE OF THE ABOVE

A popular urban myth is that Coca Cola invented Santa Claus, but the truth is that he was popular in the USA from the early 19th century. It's a coincidence that his red suit resembles Coca Cola's corporate colours.

Q68: A. TRAVEL BY HORSE

This Act, which has not yet been repealed, required everyone to attend church on Christmas Day on foot.

Q69: B. A CHRISTMAS CARD IN A RED ENVELOPE

Sending red Christmas cards to anyone in Japan constitutes bad etiquette, since funeral notices there are customarily printed in red.

Q70: B. SOUTH KOREA

Although the secular celebration of Christmas is popular in all these countries, especially Japan, South Korea is the only one that celebrates it with a national holiday.

Q71: D. A SPIDER WEB

An artificial spider and web are often included in the decorations on Ukrainian Christmas trees. A folktale tells of a poor family who found a web on their tree on Christmas morning. At daylight it turned into gold and silver.

Q72: C. 'BAH CHRISTMAS'

After *A Christmas Carol*, Charles Dickens wrote several other Christmas stories, one each year, but none was as successful as the original.

A VERY PECULIAR HISTORY
QUIZ BOOKS

OTHER TITLES IN THIS SERIES:

EGYPTIAN MUMMIES
LONDON
BRIGHTON
SCOTLAND
KINGS AND QUEENS

A VERY PECULIAR HISTORY

TITLES IN THIS SERIES:

WILLIAM SHAKESPEARE	TITANIC
SCOTTISH CLANS	THE TUDORS
SCOTTISH WORDS	SCOTLAND VOLUME I
SCOTTISH TARTAN	SCOTLAND VOLUME 2
ROBERT BURNS	LONDON
CHARLES DICKENS	CASTLES
THE 60S	IRELAND
FISHING	BRIGHTON
CRICKET	CHRISTMAS
GOLF	VAMPIRES
WHISKY	ANCIENT EGYPT
THE OLYMPICS	WALES
WORLD WAR ONE	GLOBAL WARMING
WORLD WAR TWO	RATIONS
QUEEN ELIZABETH II	THE BLITZ
VICTORIAN SERVANTS	KINGS AND QUEENS
YORKSHIRE	GREAT BRITONS

www.salariya.com
where books come to life!